10/95

A Discovery Biography

Robert E. Lee

—◆—

Hero of the South

by Charles P. Graves
illustrated by Nathan Goldstein

CHELSEA JUNIORS

A division of Chelsea House Publishers
New York ◆ Philadelphia

For Kitty and Bill Shands

The Discovery Biographies have been prepared under the educational supervision of Mary C. Austin, Ed.D., Reading Specialist and Professor of Education, Case Western Reserve University.

Cover illustration: Robert Caputo

First Chelsea House edition 1991

Copyright © MCMXCI by Chelsea House Publishers, a division of Main Line Book Co. All rights reserved.
Printed and bound in the United States of America.
© MCMLXIV by Charles P. Graves

   3 5 7 9 8 6 4 2

ISBN   0-7910-1462-2

Contents

Robert E. Lee: Hero of the South

Chapter *1*

Washington's Footsteps

"Tell us a story, Father," six-year-old Robert E. Lee begged. "Tell us what you did in George Washington's army."

"Tell us about the time you captured Paulus Hook," Robert's older brother, Smith, pleaded.

"You boys know all my war stories by heart," their father said smiling.

"But we never get tired of hearing them," Robert said. Robert was proud of his father. He knew that his father had been a hero in the Revolution.

General Lee had been given the nickname "Light-Horse Harry" because he had led a part of the cavalry. He had fought the English in New York and New Jersey. He had fought them in South Carolina and Georgia. He had been at Yorktown with Washington when the English surrendered.

When Washington died, General Lee wrote some famous words about him. He said that Washington was *"first in war, first in peace and first in the hearts of his countrymen."*

That had been a long time ago. Now Light-Horse Harry Lee was living in Alexandria, a town on the Potomac River near Washington, D.C.

"Let's take a walk," General Lee said. "I want to talk to you boys."

It was a warm day in 1813. The old soldier took Robert by one hand and Smith by the other. They walked together through the tree-lined streets of Alexandria.

"What do you want to talk to us about, Father?" Robert asked.

"I've decided to go to the West Indies," General Lee began. "I haven't been well and perhaps I'll get my health back there."

"Please may I go with you, Father?" Robert asked.

"You must stay here and go to school, son. You must help take care of your mother."

Just then they passed a church.

"That is where George Washington went to church," Robert's father said.

"Many times he walked right where we're walking now."

"Then we're walking in George Washington's footsteps!" Robert said.

General Lee put his arms around both boys. "Be good while I'm away," he said. "I want you to be honest and always do what you believe is right. Promise me that you'll try."

"I promise," Smith said.

"I promise too," Robert said.

"George Washington once told me that people should not only be honest," their father said. "People should appear honest too. You boys remember that."

A short time later General Lee went to the West Indies. Robert never saw him again. But he never forgot what his father said that day.

Chapter *2*

A Drive to Arlington

After General Lee left home Mrs. Lee was busy bringing up her family. She had three other children besides Smith and Robert. They were Carter, Ann and a baby named Mildred.

Robert's mother told him that the Lees had lived in Virginia for 150 years. They had always been leaders.

Two Lees had signed the Declaration of Independence. They had helped form the United States of America. Robert's father had been a governor of Virginia.

When Robert was a boy, Virginia was a very important state. Virginia had been the first permanent English colony in America. Now it had more people than any other state. Four out of the first five Presidents of the United States came from Virginia.

Robert E. Lee was born in Virginia on January 19, 1807, in a big house named Stratford Hall. Now Stratford Hall belonged to his half-brother, Henry. Robert often went there to visit.

Robert loved to ride his brother's horses over the rolling green fields.

Rabbits darted ahead as he raced along. The creeks and rivers sparkled like silver in the sunshine.

"Virginia must be the most beautiful place in the world," Robert thought.

When he was home in Alexandria, Robert's favorite sport was swimming. He and his friends spent many happy hours splashing in the Potomac River.

But there wasn't much time for fun. When Robert was eleven his father died. Robert's brother, Carter, had already left home. Smith was planning to join the Navy. Soon Robert was the only man in the house.

Mrs. Lee was often sick. Robert's big sister, Ann, was not well either. Robert had to help run the house.

He learned to care for the horses.

He had to keep the yard neat and he planned the meals. Robert was a good manager. He learned how to make a little go a long way. He learned to hide his feelings too. His mother never knew the times he gave up picnics with his friends to stay with her and Ann.

One spring day Mrs. Lee asked Robert to drive her to Arlington Hall in their old coach. Arlington Hall was a big plantation a few miles up the river. It was owned by the Custis family. Mrs. Custis had invited Mrs. Lee and Robert to tea.

The Lees' coach was old and had some big cracks in it. A stiff breeze was blowing and the wind whistled through the cracks.

"I'm cold, Robert," Mrs. Lee said.

Robert stopped the coach and got a newspaper. He stuffed the paper in the largest cracks. Now his mother was more comfortable.

"You're a good boy, Robert," she said.

Robert always had fun at Arlington Hall. Mary Custis was a year younger than he was. She was a step great-granddaughter of George Washington.

"I know you didn't come to see me," Mary teased Robert as they had their tea. "You just came to see George Washington's things. I asked Mother to use his china today. I hope you've noticed."

Robert's face grew red, but he was pleased. Washington was still his great hero.

After tea Robert and Mary took a walk. The dogwood was in bloom and Arlington was beautiful. Robert talked about his plans for the future.

Robert was studying at the Alexandria Academy. Arithmetic was his best subject. He wanted to go to college. But college cost a great deal of money.

"I'm going to try to get into the Military Academy at West Point," Robert told Mary. "West Point is free. Besides, it's the place I really want to go."

The United States Army educated its officers at West Point. Robert had always wanted to be a soldier.

"We'll miss you if you go there," Mary said. "But I hope you get in. I know it's what you want."

It was not easy to get into West Point. Only a few boys from each state were admitted each year.

Mrs. Lee asked Robert's relatives to help him. They wrote letters to the Secretary of War saying that Robert was a fine young man.

One morning Robert found a letter in the mailbox from the Secretary of War. His hands shook with excitement as he ripped it open. The letter said he could go to West Point.

"Hurrah!" he shouted as he ran to tell his mother. The next day Robert went to Arlington Hall to tell Mary Custis the good news.

Chapter *3*

West Point

Robert went to West Point in June, 1825. Classes would not start until September. Robert and the other new cadets spent the summer learning to be soldiers.

One of Robert's best friends was Jack Mackay. They lived in the same tent.

The boys also had the same drill instructor. He was a tough man. His first job was to teach the cadets in his squad how to stand at attention.

"Keep your heels as close together as possible," he said. "Let your arms hang naturally with your elbows near your body. No! No! Not that way! This way!"

The instructor snapped smartly to attention. Robert and Jack tried hard. They were awkward at first.

"Keep the little fingers back and touching the seams of the pantaloons," the instructor went on. "Keep the face well to the front and the eyes on the ground at fifteen paces. All right, let's try it. Squad! 'TENSHUN!"

Robert did exactly as he had been told. His heels made a sharp "click" as they snapped together. He smiled proudly.

"Mister Lee!" the instructor roared.

"Wipe that smile off your face! Throw it down on the ground and stamp on it! Don't ever let me see you smile while at attention again."

After Robert and the other cadets learned to stand at attention they were taught to march.

Hour after hour, day after day, they drilled. "One, two, three, four!" the instructor shouted. "Watch your arm swing, Mister Lee! Get in step, Mister Mackay!"

When night came they fell asleep as soon as they closed their eyes. They slept on the ground. They were so tired that it felt like a feather bed.

Slowly they became better soldiers. They were given rifles and were taught how to fire them.

One night they were told to report for guard duty.

"I've heard that the older cadets like to play jokes on new guards," Jack Mackay told Robert. "We'll probably have a busy night."

Jack was placed in one spot and Robert in another. They were told to look into anything they saw or heard.

Robert heard a loud noise on his right. "Halt!" he shouted. "Who is there?"

A shrill, mocking voice answered, "The President of the United States and two green elephants." A laugh followed. Robert was supposed to say, "Advance and be recognized." But he knew some older cadets were playing a joke on him.

He heard another noise on his left and again cried, "Halt! Who is there?"

"The King of England, five warships and two wild Indians!" The speaker had a strong Southern drawl.

"That sounds like Jeff Davis," Robert said to himself. Davis was a high-spirited cadet from Mississippi. He was always playing jokes and getting into trouble.

When Robert came off duty he found Jack in their tent.

"I was attacked by a whole army of ghosts," Jack said with a grin. "I have a good idea that the ghosts were cadets wearing sheets."

Classes began in September. Robert studied hard. He knew this was his only chance to get a good education.

The rules were strict. Many cadets broke the rules, but not Robert E. Lee. During his four years at West Point he did not get a single demerit. Jeff Davis got more than 100.

Robert's conduct was so perfect that the other cadets nicknamed him the "Marble Model." They meant that only a statue could be so perfect.

But they liked the "Marble Model." Robert's classmates were glad when he was made their highest officer in their last year. This was the finest honor a cadet could receive.

Chapter *4*

The Mexican War

Robert graduated from West Point number two in his class. This made his mother proud and happy. Mary Custis was happy too. She and Robert were in love. Soon there was a big wedding at Arlington Hall.

Robert's army work took them to many places. But he and Mary came back to visit her family whenever they could. Later Arlington Hall belonged to them. Their seven children called Virginia their home.

"This house is one round of whooping, coughing and teething," Lee said.

Mary caught the mumps from the children.

"My goodness!" Robert cried. "Didn't you have mumps when you were little?"

"I didn't have brothers and sisters to catch mumps from," Mary said.

Robert loved his children. He always missed them when he was away from home. He had to be away a great deal.

He was now a captain. He had been a soldier for many years. But he had never been in a war.

In 1846, the United States and Mexico quarreled over their boundary line. The quarrel became a war. Lee was ordered to go and served under General Winfield Scott.

General Scott decided to attack the Mexicans at Vera Cruz, an important seaport. Scott put his army on ships. Captain Lee sailed on one of the ships.

The Americans landed a few miles from Vera Cruz. Lee helped put the cannons in places where they could bombard Vera Cruz. The Americans shelled the city. It surrendered.

Now the Americans marched toward Mexico City. A big Mexican army blocked the way. Captain Lee was sent out to explore the ground ahead. He was to find the best place to attack.

A soldier named John Fitzwalter went with Lee. The two men tried not to make any noise as they hiked along. They never knew when they might run into some enemy soldiers.

They came to a spring. Lee bent down for a drink. Suddenly he heard Mexican voices. He jumped to his feet.

"Don't run!" he whispered to John Fitzwalter. "The Mexicans would hear us. We'll have to hide."

"Where?" Fitzwalter asked.

Lee pointed to a small rock a few yards away. There was room for only one man to hide behind it. Fitzwalter quickly got behind the rock.

The Mexicans were coming closer. Lee looked around. He saw a big log near the spring. Just as the Mexicans came into view he hid behind the log.

Some of the Mexicans sat down on the log. Lee was almost afraid to breathe. If the Mexicans saw him they might shoot him.

The Mexican soldiers drank from the spring. Finally they went away. Lee slowly raised his head above the log. Then he saw more Mexican soldiers coming toward the spring. He ducked behind the log again.

Mexican soldiers came and went all day long. Lee was hungry and thirsty. But he had to stay behind the log.

When it got dark the last Mexicans left. No others came. Lee got up and stretched. He called Fitzwalter. They both drank from the spring. Then they went back to the American Army and told the leaders what they had seen.

Lee learned a lot about fighting during the Mexican War. General Scott said he was a fine soldier. Lee was promoted to colonel.

A few years after the war Lee was made head of the Military Academy at West Point. This was a big job.

"When I was a cadet," Lee said to Mary, "I never thought I would be head of the Academy."

Lee tried to be fair to all the cadets. Once two of them got in a fight on the parade ground. Their names were Green and Gracie. After the fight was over, Green sneaked away. Gracie was caught. He would not tell Lee who the other cadet was.

The next day Green came to see Lee. He said that he had been the other cadet in the fight. Lee admired him for telling the truth.

"You know you can be punished for fighting," Lee said.

"Yes, sir," Green said. "But it was as much my fault as it was Gracie's. I'm ready to take what's coming."

Lee smiled. "I won't punish either of you," he said. "But don't you think it is better for friends to live in peace?"

"Yes, sir," Green agreed. "If we were all like you it would be easy."

It was acts such as this that made Lee popular with the cadets. He was head of the Academy for two and a half years. He made it better than it had ever been before. Now Lee was one of the most important officers in the United States Army.

Chapter *5*

The Road to Civil War

After Lee left West Point he had other important army jobs. He served in Kentucky, Missouri, Kansas and Texas. In Texas he helped protect the people from the Indians.

Lee began to wonder if Americans might need protection from each other. The people of the United States were quarreling. They disagreed about many things.

Most Southerners believed in slavery. Most Northerners thought slavery was wrong.

Lee felt it was wrong too. *"Slavery is a moral and political evil,"* he said.

Many Southerners believed in "States' Rights." They said they did not have to obey federal laws that went against state wishes. They felt that the states belonged to the Union by choice only.

"A state has the right to leave the Union if it wants to," these people said.

Northerners disagreed. "The Union is stronger than any state," they said. "The Union is indivisible. We must preserve it."

Lee loved the Union. He had served in the United States Army for years. But he loved his native Virginia too.

He felt his first loyalty was to Virginia.

He hoped that Virginia would not leave the Union. Then he would not have to choose between Virginia and the United States.

"I wish for no other flag than the Star-Spangled Banner," he said.

One morning in 1859, Lee was ordered to report to the Secretary of War in Washington.

"I have some terrible news," the Secretary said. "Some men are trying to steal army rifles at Harper's Ferry."

The raiders planned to give the rifles to the slaves. They hoped the slaves would kill their masters.

The Secretary of War ordered Lee to take some marines to Harper's Ferry and capture the raiders.

When Lee reached Harper's Ferry he found that the raiders had locked themselves in a building. Lee organized an attack. His men broke into the building. Several men on both sides were killed. The leader of the raiders, John Brown, was captured and put in prison.

There was no trouble with the slaves. They had not wanted the army rifles. However, the Southerners were afraid. They believed Northerners had helped John Brown. They feared there would be more trouble. Other Northerners might urge the slaves to kill their masters too.

The Southerners hated John Brown. Many of them were happy when Brown was hanged for treason and murder.

In the North John Brown became a hero. People sang, *"He's gone to be a soldier in the army of the Lord, his soul is marching on."*

John Brown's raid was the cause of more hatred between the Northerners and the Southerners.

The next year Abraham Lincoln was elected President of the United States. He was a Northerner. Soon after his election some Southern states seceded from the Union. They formed a new nation. They called it the Confederate States of America.

President Lincoln said the Southern states did not have the right to secede.

"Our fathers fought to create this great nation," he said. "We must not let it fall apart."

Lee was afraid this meant war. He prayed that Virginia would not secede.

"If I fight for the Union," he said to himself, "Virginia will call me a traitor. If I fight for Virginia, the Union will call me a traitor."

Fighting started on April 12, 1861. A few days later Lee went to meet a friend of Lincoln's in Washington.

"The President wants you to lead a Union army against the South," Lincoln's friend said.

Lee did not hesitate. "I cannot do it. If Virginia leaves the Union I must share the miseries of my people."

Later Lee went to see General Scott, his commanding officer in the Mexican War. Scott had been born in Virginia too, but he was loyal to the Union.

"What did you say to Lincoln's friend?" Scott asked.

"I said *no!* I cannot fight against Virginia."

"You have made the greatest mistake of your life," Scott said. *"The contest may be long and severe. But eventually the issue must be in favor of the Union."*

Lee's face was clouded with sorrow as he slowly rode back to Arlington. He gazed at the unfinished Washington monument. It looked like a broken pencil standing on end.

"The nation that Washington helped build is splitting in two," Lee thought. "Perhaps his monument will never be finished. I'm glad Washington can't see America now."

The next day Lee heard that Virginia had voted to secede. Sadly, he wrote a letter and resigned from the United States Army.

As he wrote he remembered the promise he had made to his father. "I am doing what I believe is right," Lee said to himself.

Chapter 6

Lee Saves Richmond

The capitol of the Confederate States was moved from Alabama to Richmond, Virginia. This made Richmond the South's most important city. Lee was there doing all he could to build an army to defend the South.

The president of the Confederate States was Jefferson Davis. He had been at West Point with Lee.

President Lincoln sent a big army into Virginia. He thought that the war would end quickly if Richmond were captured.

The Northern army was stronger than the Southern army. The North had more men, more money and more factories for making guns and bullets. But the Southern army had a lot of spirit.

"Why, one Southerner can lick 20 Yankees," the Confederates bragged.

The Northern army came closer and closer to Richmond. The Confederates tried to block their way.

The Northern soldiers got so close to Richmond that they could see the church spires. It seemed as if nothing could stop them.

Then President Davis made a wise move. He made Robert E. Lee the commander of the soldiers fighting to save Richmond.

Lee made plans to trap the Northern army. Secretly he sent word to General Stonewall Jackson to bring his army to Richmond.

Lee ordered Jackson to strike the Northern army on its right side. Then he sent three divisions to hit the Northerners in front.

This was a risky thing to do. Lee was dividing his forces. But he knew he had to take chances. His daring plan worked. The two parts of Lee's army acted like a giant nutcracker. The Northerners had to retreat or be crushed.

The Northern army fell back from the city. Richmond was saved.

Now the South had a great hero. The name "Robert E. Lee" was on the lips of all Southerners.

"What do you think of General Lee?" a man asked Stonewall Jackson.

"I would follow him blindfolded," Jackson said.

Chapter 7

Lee's Greatest Victory

Lee won many other battles. In each battle many Southern soldiers were killed. Many Northerners were killed too. The battlefields were covered with dead soldiers wearing Confederate gray and Union blue uniforms.

Lee decided to carry the fight to the North. He did not want to conquer the North. But he thought that a Southern victory on Northern land might force the North to make peace.

He led his army across the Potomac River into Maryland. He rode his horse, Traveller. Lee loved this fine, high-spirited animal who shared his dangers and hardships.

"He's Confederate gray," Lee would say to his friends. "My horse matches my uniform!"

Seated on Traveller, Lee watched as a soldier climbed up on the Maryland bank of the river. "I've rejoined the Union," the soldier said.

Lee smiled at the joke. But it was a long time before he could smile again.

He had made plans to defeat the Northern army in Maryland. One of his officers lost a copy of the plans. Northern soldiers found it. They knew exactly what Lee planned to do.

A big battle was fought at Antietam Creek. Lee's army was greatly outnumbered. Many of his men were barefoot and hungry. But they fought hard. The Northerners could not drive them back. After the battle Lee's army was too weak to go forward. It was forced to retreat.

Lee watched his men cross the river again. If the Union army attacked now, many more Southerners would die.

As the last of his soldiers got safely across Lee said, "Thank God."

The next year Lee won his greatest victory. This was at Chancellorsville in Virginia.

Lee had about 60,000 men. The Union army had 130,000. Lee was outnumbered more than two to one.

Lee showed what a great and daring general he was. He divided his army into three parts. He left one part at Fredericksburg. Then he took another part to Chancellorsville where the big Northern army was camped. He gave General Stonewall Jackson more than half of these soldiers.

"Go around the right of the Northern army," Lee told Jackson. "Hit them by surprise."

Quickly and secretly Jackson moved his men. As his soldiers attacked they gave the rebel yell.

"Woh-who-ey! Who-ey!"

It was a high, shrill scream. Many Northerners dropped their rifles and ran.

Lee and his soldiers attacked the Northern army at another place.

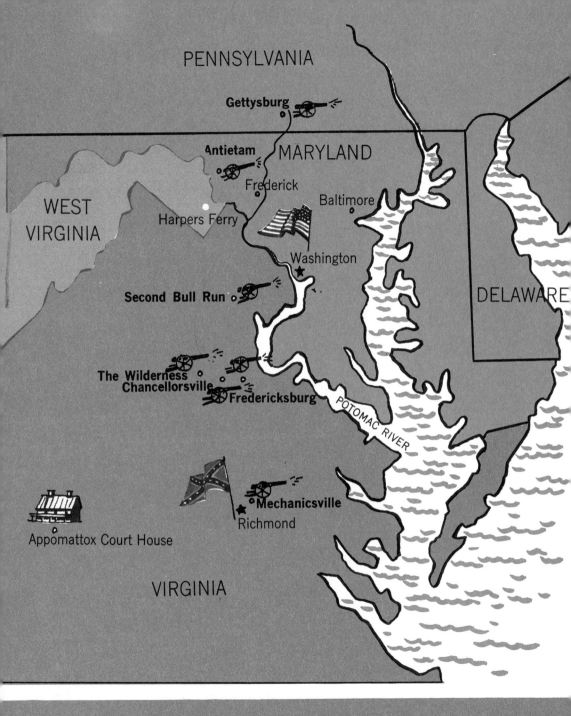

Some of Lee's Battles, 1862-1865

"Woh-who-ey!" the Southern soldiers screamed amid the smoke and flame of battle. They chased the Northerners into Chancellorsville. Shells had set the town on fire.

It was a great Confederate victory. But what a price was paid! General Stonewall Jackson was mistaken for a Northerner by his own soldiers. They shot him three times. He died within a week.

When Lee heard the news he was overcome with grief. "I have lost my right arm," he said sadly.

Chapter 8

Gettysburg

Lee knew that time was on the side of the North. The North was getting stronger every day. The South was getting weaker.

Every time a Northerner was killed there were other men ready to take his place. When a Southern soldier was killed there was no one to take his place.

The North ruled the seas. Northern ships would not let guns and food into the South from other countries.

Lee decided to invade the North again. "We must attack them before they get too strong," he said. Lee's men sang as they marched to Pennsylvania.

"I'll place my knapsack on my back,
My rifle on my shoulder,
I'll march away to the firing line
And shoot that Yankee soldier."

At Gettysburg they met a Union army led by General George Meade. For two days the armies fought like tigers. Many brave men were killed. Neither side seemed to be winning.

On the third day Lee ordered General George Pickett to punch a hole in the Northern line. Pickett had 15,000 men.

It was a hot day. Pickett's soldiers were lying in the shade resting. They heard the sound of horses' hoofbeats and looked up. Pickett was riding by with Lee.

The soldiers had been ordered not to cheer for Lee. The cheers might tell the enemy where Lee was. They might shell the area and kill him.

But as Lee rode up the men leaped to their feet. They lifted their caps in a silent cheer.

"To your posts!" Pickett ordered. "Get ready to fight!"

Lee watched Pickett's charge through his field glasses. He saw the brave Southerners rush forward, with their bayonets gleaming in the sun. Their battle flags waved above them.

Suddenly, the Northern army seemed to burst into flame. Rifles cracked. Cannons thundered. Gaps appeared in the moving Southern line as men fell like toy soldiers. Their comrades who were not hurt rushed on.

"Woh-who-ey!" they screamed. The wild battle cry struck terror in the hearts of Northern soldiers. They knew how bravely the Southerners fought. But the Northern soldiers were brave too.

"Fire!" their commander ordered. "Fire!" The Northern soldiers pulled the triggers of their rifles. Crack! More Southerners stumbled and fell, screaming with pain. Soon the ground was red with their blood.

The few Southerners who were not killed or wounded could not go on.

They turned and ran back toward their own lines. Pickett's charge had failed.

It was hard for Lee to see through the smoke. But he knew the Northerners had won the battle.

"This has been my fight," he said, *"and upon my shoulders rests the blame."* Lee always gave his men the credit for victories. But he took the blame for defeats.

Lee praised Pickett's men. "It was a grand charge," he said. *"I never saw troops behave more magnificently."*

There was nothing left for Lee to do but retreat to Virginia. He was afraid that the Northern army might chase him. But many brave Northerners had been killed and wounded. Lee got his army safely across the Potomac.

The tired Southerners rested by the peaceful riverbank. At night Lee sat by his tent looking at the flickering campfires. He could hear some of the soldiers singing.

"All quiet along the Potomac tonight,
  Where the soldiers lie peacefully
    dreaming,
  Their tents in the rays of the clear
    autumn moon,
  O'er the light of the watch fires are
    gleaming."

Lee smiled sadly. It was still a long time until autumn.

"I hope," he said to himself, "that it's as quiet in Virginia then as it is now."

Chapter *9*

The Wilderness

Virginia was not quiet again for a long time. There were many more battles. Lee's army was pushed slowly back toward Richmond.

Lincoln put a new general in charge of his armies. He was Ulysses S. Grant. Grant was a good general and he had a strong army. He was determined to win the war.

Grant moved his army into a gloomy area called the Wilderness. He planned to slip around Lee's army and capture Richmond.

The Wilderness was almost a jungle of trees and bushes and vines. Lee thought that Grant could not use all his men in such rough country. Lee decided to attack.

But nothing could stop Grant's army. They fought with all their might. Lee's soldiers were greatly outnumbered. Some of them started to run. It looked like a panic.

Lee rode among his soldiers, trying to rally them. Suddenly, he saw a group of Southern soldiers rushing forward. They were heading for the Northerners.

Lee stopped them. "Who are you, my boys?" he asked.

"We're Texas boys," one of them said.

"Hurrah for Texas!" Lee shouted. "Follow me!"

Lee dug his spurs into Traveller's flanks. He planned to lead the brave Texans into battle.

But the Texans knew that Lee might be killed. If he were killed, there would be no general to take his place.

"Go back, General Lee! Go back!" the Texans cried.

Lee kept riding forward. The Texans slowed down.

"We won't fight unless you go back," one of them said. "The whole South needs you."

Lee pulled on Traveller's reins and went back to his headquarters.

Thousands of soldiers were killed in the battle of the Wilderness. Neither side won the battle. Lee hoped that Grant would retreat.

But Grant didn't think of retreating. He marched his army to Spotsylvania, which was even closer to Richmond. Lee moved to block him and another battle was fought.

After each battle Lee's army was weaker. Grant's army got stronger and stronger.

Lee was afraid that the Southern cause was doomed. But he fought on and on and on.

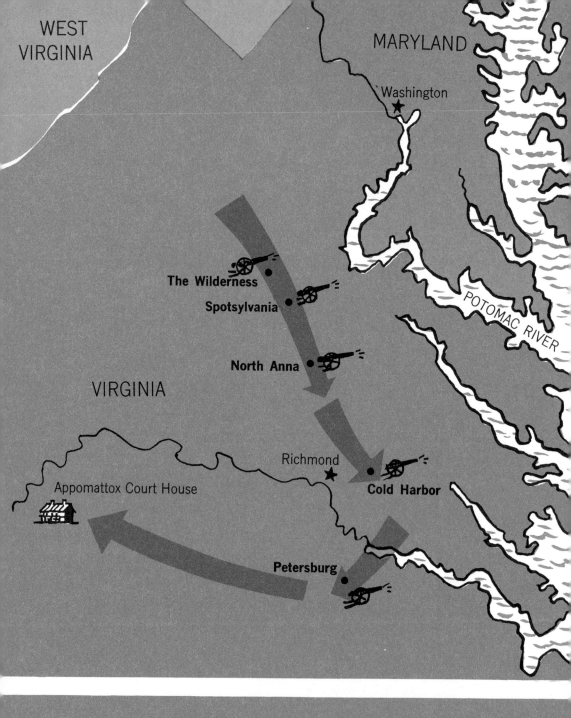

WEST VIRGINIA

MARYLAND

Washington

POTOMAC RIVER

The Wilderness

Spotsylvania

North Anna

VIRGINIA

Richmond

Cold Harbor

Appomattox Court House

Petersburg

General Lee's Last Battles, 1864-1865

Chapter *10*

Surrender

In the spring of 1865, Grant's army captured Richmond. Lee's small army retreated farther into Virginia. Grant knew that he would have to follow Lee to make him surrender.

Lee was determined not to give up unless he had to. His soldiers were hungry. Many were barefooted. They were almost out of bullets and shells. But they had their general.

"Lee gives us a big advantage," his men thought.

But this time Lee's military skill was not enough. Grant had Lee's army almost surrounded. Lee ordered one of his generals to try to break through Grant's lines.

The general tried and failed. A messenger reported to Lee. "The general has fought his men to a frazzle," the messenger said. "He cannot break the lines unless you send help."

Lee had no help to send. *"There is nothing left for me to do but go and see General Grant. And I would rather die a thousand deaths."*

He arranged to meet Grant in a farmhouse at the village of Appomattox Court House.

As he rode toward the farmhouse he wondered if Grant's terms would be harsh. If Grant wished he could march Lee's soldiers to prison camps. It might be years before they would be freed.

Lee reached the farmhouse before Grant. He went in. Soon he heard a clatter of hoofbeats outside. The door swung open and Grant entered. The two generals shook hands.

Lee told Grant that he wanted to surrender his army. He asked what the terms would be. Grant said he would let the Southern soldiers return home.

Lee sighed with relief. His men wouldn't go to prison. Then he asked Grant if his soldiers could take their horses home. He told Grant the men would need the animals for farm work.

Grant promised that all Confederate soldiers who owned horses or mules could take them home.

"This will have the best possible effect upon my men," Lee said.

Grant learned that Lee's soldiers had almost nothing to eat. He said he would send food to the hungry men at once.

The surrender terms were written on a piece of paper. Lee and Grant signed it.

They shook hands again. Lee went outside and mounted Traveller. He rode slowly back to his brave and beaten men.

Tears streamed down the faces of many Southern soldiers when they saw General Lee.

Lee took off his hat and turned to the ragged little army. "Men," he said, "I have done the best I could for you. Go to your homes." He tried to say more, but there were tears in his eyes. "Good-by," he whispered.

A few days later General Lee rode to Richmond on Traveller.

In Richmond, many Southern soldiers came to see Lee. He advised them all to become good citizens of the United States and to build back their farms.

"I believe it to be the duty of everyone to unite in the restoration of the country and the reestablishment of peace and harmony," he wrote.

Lee was pleased when he was made president of Washington College at Lexington, Virginia.

"Education can do much to rebuild the South," he said. "And it can help Northern boys and Southern boys to become friends again."

It was almost like the old days when he was head of West Point. Lee was firm but fair with all the students. The boys loved him.

Lee died in 1870. The next year Washington College became Washington and Lee University. Lee's name was forever tied to that of his childhood hero.

Today Lee is remembered as a brave soldier and a fine general. In both the North and the South, Robert E. Lee is honored as a man who always did what he thought was right.